MW01531210

Why Didn't You Know?

BY

RUTH HANCOX

Published 2019
Atlanta, GA USA

Publisher's note: This is a work of Non-Fiction. All events 'are
True to life.

Dedication

This book is dedicated to my daughters, Ruth Lloyd, Ieshia Hancox, Renika Hancox and to my sons Irving Lloyd, and Ricochet Lamar-Hancox. Also dedicated to Marquita Gallaway and in loving memory to Catherine Hancox

To my little sister, De Shane, I apologize with the sincerity of my heart for everything that I've put you through. I didn't know, my pain was also your pain, and I hurt your because I hurt. One day, maybe you can find it in your heart to forgive me.

Table of Contents

Prologue

> *Exodus 2 – 6: And when she had opened it, she saw the child. And behold the babe wept and she had compassion on him and said this is one of the Hebrew children*

My mother, Lottie Mae Ross, was a young black girl who lived in Arora, IL. She had 11 sisters and brothers, and in her young teens, due to her drug addiction, she became a ward of the state of Illinois. At age 15, she gave birth to me and named her new baby girl Ruth. Because she could not handle raising a child from inside a juvenile detention center, I was immediately taken away from her. I was then placed in an orphanage of the state and stayed there until I was 3 months old.

A young white couple saw me there and wanted to take me home. They, unfortunately, knew nothing about caring for a child. Their only motive was to collect the money I would bring to them each month for having me in their home. I was neglected throughout the entire time that I stayed with them. However, just before payment each month, they'd dress me up and clean up the house to prepare for a visit from my caseworker. It looked as though I was in the best of care. It

worked for only 3 months until a bright young woman noticed something very wrong with me.

Her name was Ms. Harmon and on this particular occasion, she wanted to hold me for a moment. I was crying loudly, and she wanted to soothe me a little before giving me back to the couple. As she began to pick me up, she noticed that I was covered with diaper rash from head to toe. This was unacceptable to her. She quickly removed me from the home, but the only option she had was to take me back to the orphanage. The thought of this was heartbreaking to her, so she elected instead to see if there could be someone out there who would accept me into their home temporarily.

Ms. Harmon discovered that there was a file on a couple named Harrison and Catherine Hancox. They already had several foster care children, so she decided that they would be suitable enough to possibly take care of me until she could find a more permanent solution. She began approaching them about fostering me and they agreed. This is where my story begins. My name is Ruth Hancox and I entered the home of Harrison and Catherine Hancox at the age of 3 months

Chapter One: The Hancox Household

Mathew 18-5: Whoever receives one such child in my name receives me."

Ms. Harmon walked up to the steps of the house nervously. I was wrapped in her arms crying because I was still covered with diaper rash. Ms. Harmon wasn't sure if I'd be excepted because of this but she had to try. She knocked on the door and a beautiful black woman opened the door. She was kind of tall, big-boned, and fair-skinned. She wasn't light but she had a light shade to her. she was wearing glasses with pointed ends with 2 diamonds embedded inside. They were called "Cat Glasses" in those days. She had beautiful salt and pepper hair which was very fine and full-bodied. She took one look at the crying baby in Ms. Harmon's arms, then she reached out to take hold of me.

"Oh, she's so beautiful. Give her to me." Catherine said.

Harrison was standing deeper in the shadow of the doorway and he smiled as his wife took the child and turned to walk inside the house. Catherine didn't even look up as he greeted Ms. Harmon and asked her to come inside. He knew that it was over. There was no further discussion needed. I was now a new member of the Hancox household and the only thing left to do was to sign the papers. Ms. Harmon went over the rules and regulations of my care, and before I knew it, I was now in my new home.

"Papa, I'm gonna go inside and take care of Ruth, will you see Ms. Harmon out?" Catherine said.

"Okay, you go 'head," Harrison replied. He signed all the papers right there at the door, then said, "Ms. Harmon, thanks for everything. We'll see to Ruth now. Don't worry 'bout a thing. You take care now."

"Okay, Mr. Hancox." Ms. Harmon said, "I'll check in on you from time to time, but I'm sure everything'll be alright. You all have a blessed day."

And she was gone.

Catherine took me to the bathroom, undressed me from the itchy clothes I'd been wearing, placed me in some nice soothing warm water, then began to softly rub me down making me feel so good that I stopped crying. I could smell the baby powder she used after drying me off and I remember that smell so fondly even to this day. Then she wrapped me up in a blanket and carried me to a chair. She then sat and held me for such a long time. Even though I was too young to fully understand, I somehow knew that I was at home in her arms. I didn't cry very much after this; I was a good baby.

Catherine, now known to me as Momma, was from Huntington, WV. She was later raised in Cleveland OH until she was old enough to move to Chicago IL which is where she met Harrison. She was unable to have children of her own and when she first met her husband, she was a professional cook. After he married her, he would no

longer allow her to work outside of the home. This was true in most cases back in the 1950s.

Harrison, whom I called "Papa" along with everybody else, was born in 1890 and he worked for the railroad until he was able to retire from it. He was born in Mark Tree, AK then moved to Chicago later on in life. When he and Momma met, they dated for about 5 years before finally getting married. Even though he was a 'ladies' man' and played the field throughout their relationship, she still married him because he was good to her and tried to give her anything she'd ask for.

He'd been widowed twice before meeting Momma, and he had children by his previous marriages which were close to Catherine's age. His children were his daughter Dorothy, who had her kids which were Winnie, June-Bug, who was in the service, Ricochet, and Larry. Papa also had two sons, Maurice, and Quin.

After Momma put up with Papa's running around and staying out all night, then coming home with the smell of perfume all over him, she knew that she had to find a way to be happy again. Back in those days, women didn't leave their husbands, and they'd put up with all sorts of things. She never thought to leave, but she did think of a way to become distracted from his wild living. Because she couldn't have children of her own, she decided to begin fostering other children. Papa, who wanted to please her, gave his permission.

Esther 1 – 20: all the wives shall give to their husband's honor both to great and small.

Being the craftsman that he was, not only did he build their home from the ground up, he began adding additional rooms to the house to accommodate the new foster children. Momma could see that he approved of this new venture of hers. It was a way to make her happy and to keep her out of his business and distracted while he continued playing the field. When she soon approached him about adopting me, he did not have any objections.

It took 2 years for the adoption to go through. Once it was done, Momma would use her own money to take care of me. The other children in the house were, Johnny, who had Polio which caused his one leg to be shorter and weaker than the other one; Andrew Lucas, who did not stay long in the house after I arrived. All I remember about him was that he had a bumpy face and was very tall. Then there was Marshall, he didn't stay in the house because he had already moved out. He would occasionally stay the night though.

Later came the girls, Marvilyn and De Shane. Those were the foster children, and money would come in for them from the state. But I was special because I was now Momma's very own child. I was known as Ruth Hancox, and I was no longer a part of the social service system. Momma poured out all the love that a mother could give onto her new baby girl. She gave me everything that I could want, and in return, she was finally fulfilled as a mother.

I was 2 years old when Marvilyn came to the house at 8 years old. Marvilyn had two long ponytails and she was

really dark-skinned with big eyes. And I thought that she was so beautiful. I thought to myself,

"Wow, I have a playmate now."

So, I ran over to touch her on her legs. Marvilyn was kind of shocked to see me do that. I wanted to make friends so, I threw a footie at her to let her know that I liked her.

"Why did you throw that sock at me? You don't want me here? You too good to have me here?" She shouted.

She was really upset about this, but I was only 2 years old and I didn't understand. I didn't know what was happening, I just wanted to play with her. But Marvilyn took offense at this, taking it the wrong way. From that day on, Marvilyn had it in for me, but I didn't know about it at the time. I always considered her my favorite sister.

Johnny, he had to walk on crutches most of the time around the house or he'd just use his arms to move around. Whenever he had to go out, like to church or school, he'd wear a leg brace. The upper part of his body was as strong as an ox because he had to carry his weight with his arms so often. But he was a very funny boy and use to always wrap his smaller leg around his neck to make us all laugh. He was a straight comedian.

When I was 4 years old, De Shane who was still an infant came to the Hancox home. She was a baby when she arrived. I couldn't play with her at first because she was too young. She had two other sisters in the foster care system who didn't live with us, and her real mother's name was Maxine Carr.

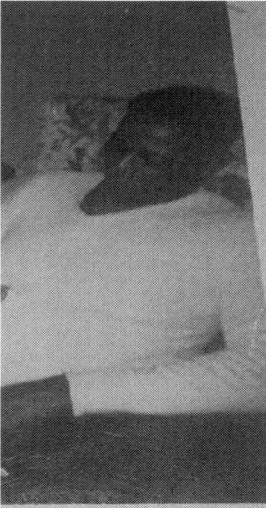

At first, Papa was good and kind to me along with the other kids. He would sit in the recliner and let me in particular brush his beautiful coal-black wavy hair. He'd tell stories about his childhood to me and the other children in the house. Stories about slavery with his parents, or how he had to pick cotton as a share-cropper. He'd tell stories about black history and how the white man was evil, or about the lies the white man told to black people about us being inferior. Or the fact that Christopher Columbus didn't discover America after all. My brothers and sisters and I would listen and learn from him about the ways of the black man's world.

Papa would play baseball with us kids and especially, he'd hit the ball for me and let me run the bases because I was so small. I really liked it when we'd do yard work together. He'd let me water the grass, or he'd push the lawnmower while I raked the leaves and pick up papers. Sometimes he'd even let me push the lawnmower, but it was too hard. And what was truly wonderful was the fact that he and Momma would let me sleep in between them in their bed at night. I felt so safe and snug. I loved being with them and I felt such love from them.

Momma and Papa used to get up early and drink coffee some mornings and I would get up with them. Papa would always get a cup for me and make us some toast to

go with it. Those were the good ole days, sitting with Momma and Papa having a cup of coffee and toast in the mornings. We'd go to church on Sundays and while driving home, Papa would let me sit on his lap and steer the car while he worked the pedals, it was so much fun.

The pastor was called Rev Keller. He baptized and christened me and I had Godparents. I would go over to my Godparents' house and eat cookies and have slumber parties. It was okay but, I thought she was a little bit mean. Her name was Mary Homen and her husband's name was Bill Homen. When I had children of my own, they did a lot for my first child Irving and when I had little Ruth, they didn't want to do too much for her because they said I had baby after baby when I only had two. So that was the end of that.

The house we lived in had an upstairs apartment, the main floor where we lived, and a basement apartment. Three families lived there, and Papa, who owned it, rented it out to the other two families. Upstairs lived Dorothy Galloway. She was Papa's child and we all called her Aunt Dot. When I was little, I remember going upstairs where she lived to play with her daughter Winnie.

Winnie was tall and light-skinned with long pretty hair. She wasn't tall and but she was taller than me. She and I got along great. Aunt Dot would be in the kitchen

cooking and drinking Pabst Blue Ribbon beer. She liked beer, she also liked to play the record player with her 33 albums, and she'd sometimes listen to the radio. She was the one who influenced me with music. Winnie and I liked playing with Ricochet and Larry also, Winnie's brothers. There were a few times Momma left me at the house with Aunt Dot who would babysit me.

Chapter Two: Growing Up

> *Proverbs 22 – 16: Train up a child in the way he should go and when he is old, he will not depart from it.*
> *Proverbs 18 – 24: a man that hath friends must shew himself friendly and there is a friend that sticketh closer than a brother.*

Up until the age of 5, for me everything was perfect. I don't know what happened on this particular night, but something was different. Momma was asleep, but I wasn't yet and I could hear Papa's breathing so I knew that he wasn't either. He reached over and grabbed my hand. Something he'd done on previous occasions, but for some reason, I didn't want to do it this time. He placed my hand on his private part. It was hard as always, but this time I

14

jerked my hand away and began kicking Momma. He grabbed it again and put it there and wanted me to rub it as usual but I kept kicking Momma until she woke up.

She saw what was happening. She grabbed me and swung me over her body to put me on the other side of her. Then she turned her back on Papa and put her arm around me and softly told me to go back to sleep. After a short while, I did. The next morning while I and my siblings were eating breakfast, Momma and Papa were shouting loud in the bedroom making us kids feel uncomfortable. None of us had ever heard such a bad argument between our parents before. I knew what it was about, but I didn't say anything to the others.

Things were wrong somehow in the house throughout that day, and that night, I was ordered into Marvilyn's room to sleep with her. I felt as though I'd been punished, but deep down inside, I knew that it wasn't my fault. After that, Papa became cold to me. It registered that things had changed between Papa and me, but the evidence of it didn't happen until that Sunday. He didn't let me steer the car home as he did normally so, we all knew something was different.

That night for dinner we had fried chicken. A favorite of the family's and especially the cat, Penny, who would get the wingtips. Papa loved the chicken legs so everyone made sure he got them. This is how this particular dinner went,

Everybody came into the dining room as usual, and we all sat down to say our bible verses. One of my bible verses

was "The Lord is my Shephard; I shall not want." That was one of my favorite bible verses that I said at the table. Momma would stand and start passing 'round a plate starting with the meat first. I was the first one to get a piece. We would pass it around the table. And as we ate, and got to the end, Momma would put vegetables on my plate, I hated vegetables. At the end of dinner, I would have all these vegetables still on my plate and all the meat would be eaten up. But on this night, Papa said,

"You gonna eat them damn vegetables."

I froze, and just sat there looking at him. He'd never said anything before.

"Okay."

"Eat 'em right now before I stuff 'em down your throat."

"Papa, I don't want 'em."

"I don't care. You're gonna eat 'em anyway. You're gonna eat everything on your plate."

"Oh, I don't wanna eat 'em. I'm full."

"Well you just sit right there at the table till you finish all your vegetables, and you can't get up. Everybody else, put your plates up. But you," He continued, looking straight at me, "cannot leave this table till you eat your vegetables."

Of course, I stuffed as much of them down as I could, but I could never eat them all. Up until this night, I got away

with not eating all my vegetables because I couldn't stand them. Papa decided that he wouldn't put up with it anymore. His rule from this point on was that everyone had to eat every bite of food on their plates. I was to no longer get away with not eating my vegetables. I had to sit at the table until every bit was gone, even if it meant that I'd stay there all night.

After a while, I tried to get up from the table, and he threatened to whoop me if I didn't sit my ass back down and eat everything on my plate. I didn't know what was going on and when he came after me, I managed to get away from him long enough for him to get tired of chasing me. He gave up, so I thought I'd gotten away with it. But that night, when I was in a deep sleep, I woke up suddenly and found out that I had been hog-tied. I looked up and there he was standing over the couch with his belt in his hand.

"Bitch, you thought you was gonna get away from me, you little heifer." He said,

"No Papa, I won't do it no more. Please, Papa!"

"Yeah, you ran through the house, but I got yo-ass now. You not gettin' the fuck away from me now are you, you slut. I'm a beat yo-ass."

With every stroke of his belt, he'd say stuff like,

"You fuckin' Bitch. You ain't nothin' but a tramp. I can't stand yo-ass. I'm a beat the hell outta you. I'm a show you who the damn boss is. You ain't no boss 'round here, you ain't nothin' but a Lil' tramp. Just a slut."

From that day on, when he'd get frustrated with me, he hog-tied me up late at night with my hands and feet tied together, then he'd whoop me until he got tired. Momma would jump in when she could and stop the beatings because she knew why they were happening, but not before he did some major damage.

Most of the time he'd use his belt or hands, but sometimes he'd use his cane when he was really angry. It was the kind that was made of wood and curved on one end with the rubber tip on the other. He'd do this after everyone was in bed. But I admit, that after a while, sometimes I got to thinking that maybe, there was a good reason for it. I didn't know any better.

I hated that I had to sleep with Marvilyn. I wanted to feel the warmth of my Momma next to me again, so I occasionally wet the bed. I didn't do it on purpose, but I was so miserable. Marvilyn acted like she didn't really like me. I noticed it, even though she was still my favorite sister.

Around the corner lived another mother who had a foster child about my age. She was the only child living in the house and previously, Momma and the child's mother talked about how lonely she was and that maybe she and I could play together. Momma was worried about me, and she wanted to take me away from all the turmoil in the Hancox house. So, both mothers decided to put us, two girls, together.

There was a sandbox behind their house so the little girl's mother invited me to come over one day. She took the

two of us out to the back of the house and put us in the sandbox together, then stepped away to see if we would get along.

"My name's Ruth, what's your name?"

"Linda."

"Do you have any friends Linda?"

"No, do you?"

"No. Wanna be friends?"

"Okay."

And that was all it took. Momma knew that Linda and I would get along just fine. From that day on Momma or Linda's mother would come and get us girls and we'd stay over-night in each other's houses. Sometime later, we met Crystal Brown who lived in the house behind our house. She'd come over, and the three of us would play together. It was a big deal one day when Momma went out and bought the new Cat-In-The-Hat book. It was the one where you could put the names of your child and their friends inside as part of the characters. Momma had me, Linda and Crystal added to the book and boy was it fun to read it with our names in it.

But Linda and I were together most often. We were like 2 peas in a pod. She was my first and best friend and it stayed like that while I was 5 and 6 years old. Another thing that brought us closer was when I told her about Marshall. He would sometimes come and stay the night

because he used to live there. A couple of times he tried to touch me, and I knew that it was wrong. Thank goodness he didn't stay there all the time. When I told Linda about it, she hugged me and told me it would be alright. I loved her for that.

Linda was a sickly child sometimes, but that didn't stop us from finding things to do together. Then one day Momma went over to Linda's mother's house and Linda wasn't there. Come to find out, Linda went back into foster care. She never came back, and it broke my heart. I didn't hear anything else about her and when I asked Momma to go find out about her, she wouldn't do it. She just left it alone and I couldn't understand why.

After Linda disappeared, I was alone again. Eventually, I became accustomed to Papa and I learned to live with the pain of his whooping's. Meanwhile, I went about the business of being just one of the siblings in the Hancox household. A year had passed since I moved into the room with Marvilyn. Then suddenly, my brother Johnny started taking an interest in me. He started taking me under his wing and teaching me about himself.

He was a very good artist and would draw some amazing things and show them to me. It was what brought us close together. He was 7 years older than me but he made me feel so special. For the first time in my life, someone other than my mother showed me a little kindness and love. His attention got me through a lot of those bad times.

Another person came into our lives from Papa's past; Aunt Emma. Momma told me that she was one of Papa's lovers. I was told later by Diane that she lived in the basement apartment before I arrived at the Hancox house. She and Papa dated for a little while but at the same time, he was dating my mother. Momma stole Papa away from Aunt Emma and she was furious about this. She tried everything in her power to break them up. But she didn't succeed. So, she got pregnant with Diane. Papa called her his god-daughter. She was 12 years older than me.

Diane was fairer skinned and looked like she could have been from the islands but she wasn't. She had very long pretty black hair, and her nose was slender. She didn't have any chest at all, just little stubbles that were growing.

What's strange is that at the same time, Aunt Emma was also dating a Mr. Hicks, and Diane may have been his daughter. She came to Papa and told him Diane was his baby, not Mr. Hick's. Papa was against it, he didn't believe Diane was his, even though she looked like him a little when she was young.

Momma told Aunt Emma that she would help her with Diane, and she started sending her boxes and things. She also told her that If she didn't stop trying to separate her and Papa, she would go to Mr. Hicks about Diane. So, because Momma helped with Diane, and because of her threat, Aunt Emma stopped trying to interfere with their lives and to separate them.

When Aunt Emma moved to California, Momma would take me there to visit her and I remember when we went to Disney Land and so many other exciting places while we were out there. Momma and Aunt Emma would visit back and forth between Chicago and California a lot, and it was so much fun.

Papa never did accept Diane as his child though, but Momma would get money from Papa and in his name, give it to Aunt Emma to help support them. They thought Papa was the one who accepted Diane and helped her, but it was all Momma's doing. Even to this day, Diane thinks that she got support from Papa but it was really Momma who did it all. But man, when we went to Disney Land, it was one of the best times I'd ever had as a child.

Another friend I had at the time was Beverly Smith. She and I went to church together. She was about 3 years older than I, and we were in the church choir together. One day I had some sunflower seeds in my pocket, Beverly reached in and grabbed my seeds and spit the shells on the floor under my chair. I almost got into trouble for it but a church lady saw what happened. Beverly and I got in a fight about it, but eventually, we became friends.

We'd go to the usher's room and steal hats and scarves and gloves. Then we'd go into the neighborhood and try to sell them in the wintertime. Sometimes we got away with it. We'd then go to the park and buy some weed and smoke it before going home. Sometimes we'd stay out and sleep in the park because we were scared to go home and get in trouble.

Before we got hip to taking the stuff from church and selling it, Beverly tried to convince me that orange and banana peels could be put in the window sill, and dried out. Then we could try to smoke them. Or we'd try to smoke regular brown grass on the ground to get high. We were so ignorant. we would choke on the grass. Beverly and I were thick as thieves. Once again, I had a friend like Linda, and we were like two peas in a pod. We would spend the night at each other's houses all the time.

Chapter Three: The Siblings

Genesis 34 – 2: And when Shechem the son of Hamor the Hivite prince of the country saw her he took her and lay with her and defiled her.

At home, things were pretty bad with Papa. I couldn't escape his anger and abuse and I thought I'd die living in that house. Then, one day, after a bad whooping from him, Johnny was riding his skateboard. He would paddle it with his hands while sitting on it with folded legs. He saw me crying and paddled up to me and started making faces at me to get me to laugh.

"What's wrong?"

"Papa."

"That's all you have to say. Well, I'm here now, wanna play with me? It'll take your mind off it."

"Sure!"

I couldn't believe it. Johnny was much older than me and he wanted to play with me. He'd never asked me before. Maybe he would be my friend now.

"Follow me." He said.

He led me to the back porch and nobody else was there. He grabbed a blue folder and took it over to the chair next to the corner and beckoned me to follow him.

"Here, sit down. I wanna show you something."

I sat down and he put the folder on my lap and opened it. Inside were the most beautiful drawings I'd ever seen. There were drawings of animals and ballerinas with lots of swirling colors and shapes. And he'd explain each one and point out different things about them. When I'd ask questions, he was so patient and I loved his voice as he explained things to me. I just loved how he treated me with such gentle care and patience. He was so special.

When he saw how much I loved being with him as he showed me his pictures and talked to me, he started asking me every day to spend time with him on the back porch. He'd let me dance for him and he'd have candy and things for me from time to time. It was the best time ever being with him. One day, he was so clever, that he took a box and cut a hole at the bottom. Then he took a lamp and placed it inside. On the other end, he'd put one of his

drawings over the tip and then he'd point the whole thing at the wall. You could see the shadows and shapes of the drawings on the wall and he'd move it to make it look like a movie for us to watch. He was such a genius.

"Okay, we're gonna do something different today," Johnny said one day.

"What?" I asked.

"Go inside and put on a dress. But don't put on any panties okay."

"Why not?"

"Because you're gonna be a ballerina and dance for me. Ballerina's don't wear panties because they have to twirl around."

"Okay."

I was so excited I ran to my room. I was going to be a ballerina and dance for Johnny. He liked it when I danced. I couldn't wait to get that dress on and go back out to the porch. We were the only ones home so this was going to be just for Johnny and me. I couldn't wait.

When I got back out on the porch Johnny said,

"Okay, you look fabulous. Now go ahead and dance for me."

I danced around him while he sat crossed-legged on the floor.

25

"Now twirl around."

I twirled around and around, liking how he was looking at me.

"Okay now, we're gonna make a TV show. Stop right there and lay down."

I stopped right in front of him and laid down. I couldn't believe he was gonna make a TV show with me.

"Okay now, you gotta pose for the camera okay. Spread your legs out wide so I can get a good picture."

He started pretending like he was taking pictures with his hands and making clicking sounds with his mouth. He moved closer and closer until he was right up to me. Then he gently started lifting my dress.

"What are you doing?" I said. It felt kind of uncomfortable.

"Don't worry. It's all part of the show. You wanna be a star on TV, right?"

"Yeah."

"You know I would never hurt you right?"

"I know that."

"Then hold still."

WHY DIDN'T YOU KNOW?   by: Ruth Hancox

He kept pretending to take pictures. He got closer and
closer. Next thing I knew, I could feel his mouth on my
private part. He started swirling his tongue around and
around all over me down there. I didn't know what was
happening but I didn't want to tell him to stop. He was
my friend now and I didn't want him to be mad at me. It
didn't hurt or anything, it kind of started feeling good. It
was Johnny, after all, he wouldn't do anything wrong to
me.

So, I let him do it as long as he wanted to. When it was
over, he just smiled and hugged me.

"You did real good little sis. I'm so proud of you. Now
you're a ballerina and we can do this all the time okay."

I was a little confused, but Johnny loved me and he was
my friend. He and I will be together all the time, that's all
I wanted.

"Okay."

This went on for quite some time. I grew to love Johnny.
He paid so much attention to me, he was the only one
who listened to me when I was sad or needed somebody
to talk to. There had been rumors about him going
around. I didn't believe it. He was my Johnny and I didn't
care what anyone said, he was good to me and had
always been good. The rumors were about the dog.

As he started growing older, he was rumored to take the
family dog and lock it into his room for days at a time.
Later it was believed that he would have sex with the dog
because when it was finally let go, the family would

notice that its butt hole was an expanded size and the dog was suffering. Momma would not allow the dog to go near him anymore and of course, she wouldn't let him take it anywhere alone. There was no way he was doing that to that dog. I didn't believe it.

I use to want to hang with Johnny and his friends but he didn't want me to because I was too young. One day I snatched Johnny's crutches and threw them over the fence and told him he couldn't go if I couldn't go with him. The neighbor lady saw him having such a hard time trying to crawl to get them back so, she gave them back to him. I was so mad at him when he wouldn't let me go, but I felt sorry afterward and I apologized. Even though this happened, we were still very close.

One night, when I was 7 years old, I walked into our bedroom and saw Marvilyn crying.

"What's wrong Marvilyn?" I asked.

"Momma won't let me go to the party. She won't give me a couple of dollars to get there and I wanna go."

"Don't worry, I'll handle it," I said, excited to be doing something for my favorite sister.

I snuck into Momma and Papa's room and grabbed Momma's pocketbook. I snatched some money from it quick then snuck back out to find Marvilyn to give it to her.

"Hear, now stop crying. You can go out of the window and Momma won't know."

Next thing I knew, Momma was calling me over to her in the living room.

"Ruth, what have you done? Marvilyn told me that you stole this money from out my pocketbook and gave it to her." She said as she pushed the money up under my nose to make sure I saw it. "Haven't I taught you anything about stealing? I didn't want Marvilyn to go to that party because it was dangerous."

When Papa got home, he gave me the whooping of my life. When I finally got back in the bedroom, Marvilyn was sleep. I was so angry with her; I couldn't understand why she turned on me like that. I didn't have a clue that she didn't like me. No one seemed to like me in the house except Momma and Johnny.

Marvilyn though used to always get beat up too. She used to run away all the time but they never reported her missing and they would get so worried about her. But she'd always come back. Once she and Papa got into it for some reason, and Papa chased her with a gun-running down 111th place shooting at her. Then he fell on the side of the fence and had a heart attack. That incident caused him to have a Pace-Maker put in.

Because she was older when she came to the house, she'd have such big problems with Papa and the sexual things. She and Papa never got along so, there was always a conflict between them. The other kids in the house would be jealous of me because I was treated differently, and the fact that I was adopted. I guess that's why she never really liked me. She finally left for the last time at age 15.

Holy shit, it hurt so bad. I started crying and making noises trying to get him to stop.

"Shhh. You gotta be quiet. We can't let anybody else hear us."

"But it hurts me."

"I know, but it'll get better, I promise. You have to stretch out that's all. It'll only take a few tries, then it'll be good. You'll enjoy it just like when I lick you. You like that don't you?"

"Yeah."

"But you didn't at first right."

"Yeah."

"Well, this is the same way. It'll hurt for a few times, then you'll like it okay. Trust me."

"Okay. But please go slow. It hurts."

It would hurt me for quite a while, but I still would allow it because by this time I'd fallen deeply in love with Johnny, and I wanted to do whatever he asked of me. He used to tell me to use Ice-cream to rinse it out so that there would be no evidence. Eventually, I grew to even tolerate this. I fell for him to the point that I would look so forward to his coming home from school each day.

I'd get home before him and would sit at the window waiting. When I'd see him coming, I'd run through the

house saying "Johnny's home, Johnny's home." Johnny and I would always be together, not understanding that what we were doing was wrong. The sex went on almost every night for about 3 years. And Johnny was right, I grew to like it just as he did.

Sometimes I was late getting up for school after Johnny had me up all night. Papa would come in and throw a pale of water on me to wake me up. Momma would run in and shout at him for it. Momma knew why things were happening to me. It all goes back to the incident in the bed, so she'd defend me more than any of the other children.

When it was raining, Momma used to take me Johnny, De Shane, and Winnie to White Castles which was popular in those days. McDonald's wasn't around yet. Eventually, Aunt Dot moved and got her own house, and Papa helped her out with moving the furniture. Me and De Shane decided to ride our bikes over to the new house. Johnny followed us riding his skateboard and it was a long ride, but we were determined to go. Once we got there, Aunt Dot called Momma and told her where we were and to come to get us because it was too far for us to go back. Especially Johnny on the skateboard. But Momma said,

"I'm not coming to get 'em, they'd better get back home the same way they got there. And they'd better be here before the streetlights come on."

So, we took some water and headed back home. We didn't even have time to play while we were there. We

had to get back before the streetlights came on and we
knew it would take the rest of the day. That was the
longest bike ride I remember ever taking. Especially
because we had to keep stopping and waiting for Johnny.
After that, sometimes Momma and Papa would take us
over there to play with them. Winnie and I would play in
her closet. She had a lot of toys, and I would love to play
with her Easy-Bake-Oven. It came on when you plugged
it in.

Then, Aunt Jean just appeared out of nowhere. When I
was about 8, she came into ours lives. She knocked on the
door and said she was from San Diego, CA. She knew all
about Papa, his full name, his home town. She said she
was papa's cousin, but Momma thought she was too
young. She had a son named Dwayne, and a daughter
named La Wanda. They moved in with us for about 2
months even though Papa said he didn't know who she
was. She could have been one of his lovers since she did
know some things about his past.

I was told to call her Auntie Jean and she was religious
but non-denominational. She tried to make Johnny walk
even though he couldn't. She said he didn't have enough
faith. She wanted the family to lay hands on him and to
use our faith to heal him. We all thought this was weird.

She had a nice Fleetwood and she took me to her church
with her. This was the first time I saw a lot of people
praying all at the same time. They would all stand up at
one time and pray together. People at my regular church
would shout and get the holy ghost and stuff like that, but
I'd never seen the laying on of hands and people falling

out on the floor like that. The preacher would heal them by pushing their foreheads back to pray out the demons. I was impressed with the church, I wanted to go all the time because it was livelier. They'd speak in tongues and pray all night long.

I got close to Auntie Jean. She and I would stay up all night talking. She knew that something was wrong between Papa and me but she never straight out asked me what it was. She'd counsel me and even though she didn't know what the truth was, she would always be there to listen and hug me when I was down. Papa was good at hiding the truth of all the pain in the house. When she left, I cried like a baby. I was begging her not to go. I wanted her to take me with her. I wanted to leave that house with them so bad. This was the time when Papa was tying me up at night, and throwing water on me in the mornings.

Shortly after Auntie Jean Left, Beverly Smith and I, who had been playing together for about 3 years now, would still get together sometimes. But then, at around age 9, her parents told her she had to play with someone older, close to her age, a girl named Elizabeth McFarlan who I couldn't stand. So, I was alone once again.

Chapter Four: Roller Skating, and School

*Proverbs 10 – 28: The prospect of the righteous is joy,
but the hopes of the wicked come to nothing
James 5 – 5: Ye have lived in pleasure on the earth, and
been wanton; ye have nourished your hearts as in a day
of slaughter.*

I did a lot of stuff by myself because I didn't have any
close friends. One of them was roller skating. There were
2 men, Mr. Glen, and Mr. Barr. They had a Bus parked
right on the side of our yard. Mr. Glen stole the parking
spot from Momma and Papa. They thought they had paid
the house tax which covered part of the land. But Mr.
Glen took it and parked his bus on it. He used to take the
kids skating for $3.00 which would allow them to get on
his bus and $5.00 to skate at the rink.

So, I would get on the bus right there in the yard, and
then he'd pick up all the other kids at Ada Park. I did this

for years on Friday nights. It was so much fun even though I didn't have any friends, I still knew how to skate, and I'd love the freedom of it all, being away from the house. There was a big skating rink, a little one, and a disco for whoever wanted to dance all at the same place. I loved to watch them dance because I didn't know how to dance myself.

Little did I know on one occasion, that my skating days would soon be over. I got dressed up to go skating and Momma told me that I had to ask Papa could I go. The lady at the rink told Momma and Papa that I needed to ask both parents' permission when I wanted to go there. I had to get the money from Papa, and it would be hard because he'd say that it was getting to be hard times in the world.

Momma used to give me $8.00 to buy food. I was always good with money and I saved. But this time, I went to Papa and asked him could I go, and he sent me right back to Momma. She said that they would get together and talk about it. I knew I wasn't going to be able to go, and I stewed about it all week long. But, Thursday night, Momma came to me and said I could go but I had to go to Papa to get the money.

I thought to myself,

"What type of foul play is this? That man hates me now, and I have to go to him to ask for the money?"

I tried to think all night about how I was going to get the money from Papa. I maybe could sneak in and steal it, but

I knew that that wouldn't work. So, I cleaned up all day around Papa. Fluffing the pillow that he had in his chair. Getting buttermilk so he wouldn't have to do anything. I was a busy little bee to make sure he was in a good mood.

The Bus leaves the house at 6:00 p.m. and it was already 5:00 p.m. So, I finally asked him, and he said,

"Yes, how much do you need?"

I said, "$8.00 would pay for my bus ride and the skating."

I watched him reached for his wallet, and he gave me a $20.00-dollar bill. I couldn't believe it! I was so happy, I could now get two pieces of pie, one for me and one for this girl who I saw there all the time. She doesn't come on the bus. I think her mother drops her off, and she looks like she's my age. I was hoping she'd be there tonight so we can eat and skate together.

When she walked in, my face lit up and it seemed like she was glad to see me too. She put on her skates and we began to skate together hard and fast using different types of steps. We skated half the night away with her in front sometimes and me in front other times. We'd sit down and I got the nerve to ask her if she would like a slice of pizza. She said yes and we ate pizza together. Then we skated the rest of the night away.

I forgot to get her name and phone # that night when it was time to go home. She ran to get in her mother's car and as she was getting in, 6 girls came at me from behind and jumped me. I didn't know who they were, they came out of nowhere. They beat me up and stole the rest of my

money. My new friend's mother and Mr. Glen jumped out and saved me, but I was never allowed to go skating again after that.

The school was a way for me to forget my problems at home, but it too was trying for me. There was this girl named Brenda Hunt. Momma used to give me money for lunch in the mornings before school. Like $2.00 every morning. I'd stop and get a dollars' worth of penny candy, a pickle, and a bag of potato chips. Brenda would see me and meet me inside the store and would try to take my candy.

"You better buy me some candy."

"What, you're kidding me, right? This is my money; I don't have to buy you anything."

"You'd better, or I'll beat the shit out of you."

"Try it."

She pushed me down and started to beat me up. I had to give in. She tore my ass up. This went on till I got smart. I started telling her that I didn't have any money. I started to save it up until Friday and because she didn't see me going to the store every day, she stopped beating me up. I was scared of Brenda.

Brenda always smelled like pee, like she peed in the bed, and her clothes were always dirty. She was big, black, and ugly. She would bully boys around too, that's how tough she was. And she had a lot of brothers and sisters so she was brave about her bullying cause she knew she

had backup if anybody messed with her. So, on Fridays, after I saved my money up all week, I would buy Karen, Brenda and myself some penny candy, and some chips and then I'd have some money left over for the weekend

This went on about 6 months until Brenda found out where I lived and would try to take my toys home. Because I was scared of her, I'd let her take whatever she wanted. Momma found out about Brenda taking my toys so, she told me to get my toys back and don't let her take any more toys out of the house. I knew I would have to fight her. She'd call me names like 'big nose' and make signs like she was going to fight me all the time.

Every day, after school, I would be in the position to run from her. It worked for a while but eventually, I got caught and I had to fight her. The first 2 times, Brenda did beat my ass. But one day at the lockers, I got fed up and mad, and I don't know how it happened, but I won a fight against her and she stopped bullying from that day on.

Then, Brenda's sister Betty told her that she'd better stop fighting me because she was gonna be my Godmother. Betty thought I was so pretty. She asked Momma if she could be my Godmother and Momma said no. But Betty still said she would be. And she protected me from Brenda. I was invited to her house to stay overnight once and I had to sleep in a bed that smelled like pee. And Brenda's brother Tee-Top made it clear that he wanted to get me after that. He would try to chase me home from school all the time but I knew all the short-cuts and was able to avoid him.

School wasn't all that bad though, I use to play with this girl named Rochelle Falls. She and I were really good friend. She was one of the prettiest girls in the class. We use to play together all the time while we went to school together. We'd also play in Ada park all the time. We use to play there even before school started.

Then there was Karen Frazier. She and I were in the 5th grade together. She was another really pretty girl. She had olive skin like a Pilipino or something She had really good hair and she may have been a Muslim because she would wear real long dresses and had to wear the turban on her head. She was teased by the boys and they treated her badly because of it. They'd snatch the turban off her head and eventually, her mother took her out of the school.

While walking home from school at the age of 10 years old, I met a guy named Atkins. He was a guy that use to sell clothes when Calvin Klein first came out and Jordash jeans was a hot item. I remember when I'd come from the candy store on the corner from where I use to stay and he was right there on the corner with all these nice pretty denim blue jeans. Atkins was dark-skinned and he was very short with a big head. And he started talking to me.

"Hey you, beautiful sister, want a pair of jeans? What size do you wear?"

"I wear a size one. You got any of those?"

"Hmm, well I don't have that size right here with me now, but I do have some five, six and sevens. Can you wear any of those?"

"No, they're too big for me."

"Well, I tell you what, I do have some ones back at the crib. I really wanna give you a pair cause you're such a pretty little thing. I see you walking all the time and I'd like to do something nice for you. You seem a little down. Wanna walk back up the street with me to get a pair?"

"Well, I don't know…"

"Look, I'm cool, I know you stay right up the street in that green house and I know your mother from way back. When you take 'em home, let her know that this time it's a gift, but the next time, she can pay for 'em. That's fair right?"

"Wow, that'd be great. Okay, that's fine, I'll walk with you." I couldn't believe he was gonna give me a free pair of jeans. This was the shit.

We began to walk down 111th street. He said he stayed close to ADA Park and when we got there, we went around to the side of the house where there was a gate.

"Go to the back and meet me at the window."

I somehow didn't think anything was wrong with that. I figured he had some people in the house and he didn't want them to know he was giving away his jeans. So, he

let me in the gate and I went to the back yard to wait at the window.

Next thing I knew, he had opened the window and pulled out a gun and aimed it at me. I guess you know what happened after that. Another experience with rape again. But this time, it was a stranger and I didn't see it coming or like it at all. It was hard and cold and he didn't give a damn. Would you believe he got scared and ended up giving me the pair of jeans after it was over? I walked home crying with the jeans wrapped in my arms. I walked into the house and told Momma that a guy gave me a pair of jeans while I was still kind of crying. That was the end of that.

Reverend Keller passed away so we got a new preacher named Reverend Ross. He didn't last too long in the church but Momma liked him. He used to go to play tennis and my Momma wanted the best for me so, she wanted me to start taking tennis lessons. This was before I left the house. I remember when I was coming down the back stairs of the church coming from the choir stand and the secretary's office, the pastor's study was behind the secretary's office. I was going down the steps and Reverend Ross met me on the steps as he was going up and I was coming down. He just stopped and started tongue kissing me right on the steps.

At this time, I was looking for him because Momma had brought me the tennis racket and she didn't know that he had mental issues when she wanted me to take lessons. He was a child molester because he fondled me right then and there and he just tongue kissed me right there in the

church. I thought to myself, Lord, I'm not even safe in the church.

So, I used to always think like, why me, is this what I was born to do. When will this ever stop, how long will my life go on with nothing but rapes with maybe a little fun in between?

All the time that all this was going on with me, it seems like Momma should have known. I was being raped not only outside the house but in the house too. She never indicated that she knew anything. She never caught on that these things happened right up under her nose. How could you not know that your daughter, whom you claimed to love so much, was suffering these assaults with friends and family members? How could she not see any signs of me being abused?

Since no one seemed to give a damn, sex to me became just another thing. Momma used to babysit a girl named Riatta Woods after school. Because of this, Riatta and I became very close friends. Then one day, her mother came over to talk to Momma regarding her husband. She was in tears saying that he had raped and fondled his daughter. Riatta had also been molested by him. Everything he did to her, she did to me.

She loved to play house and eat pussy. I learned how to give it back from Riatta. Johnny had never taught me that part. I would do the same to other kids such as Crystal and Willene Moss. But because Willene didn't like it, she told her mother. Then her mother came over and told Momma, but I didn't get into trouble because Momma

43

said that kids will be kids, and of course I didn't know any better. I didn't mean any harm. Momma would always defend me.

There was one bright light which happened around this time. Shawn, my nephew, Marvilyn's child, was left with the Hancox when he was 2 months old. Marvilyn had had him when she left home but she couldn't take care of him at the time. He slept on my chest until he was about 6 months old. I would change his diapers and sit and hold him all day after school. After about 6 months, Marvilyn came back and got him. I was so upset because I had grown so attached to him. I thought of him as my baby now, and I told Momma to make Marvilyn leave him with me. Momma explained to me that he was her baby. Next time I saw him, he was about 2 years old.

I remember a time when I came in the back room where Papa and Momma use to sleep and caught him turning up this brown looking bottle. This is before I started drinking. I asked him what it was, and he said it was used to help him with his gums. But it was actually liquor called Imperial Whiskey. So later when he wasn't there, I went in his drawer and got the bottle out and turned it up, and oh my God, it was really hot and burnt my throat going down. But I did it a few times anyway.

I continued to go in his drawer, and drink from his bottle, but at the time I didn't know it was liquor, I thought it was a medicine which would help my teeth as he told me it was. I wanted strong teeth and gums just like him.

Another thing was, Momma and Papa use to keep the holy communion for the church and I thought it was grape juice. But it was wine. All I knew is that they would take it every Sunday and Momma would take a little and put the rest back in the closet. Well, one day I went into the closet and got it and took it to my room and I had all my toys out and was serving it to myself and all my dolls. Before I knew it, I was drunk crawling around the floor. That was a sight with the wine bottle. After that, she would put the wine up, and later on, somebody else started taking it home. I know she told the church about that because they said they could imagine how funny I was, crawling around tipsy. Eventually, I even threw up because I was so drunk.

Chapter Five: San Diego & Fun

But all wasn't well. Momma noticed me sinking fast. I was getting into more trouble, Papa was whooping me endlessly, and Johnny was still having his way with me. I just didn't care anymore and she could see that. Eventually, she called Auntie Jean and offered to pay her to keep me with her in San Diego. She accepted, and for about a year while I was in the 5th grade, I was allowed to say with her there. I went to Leaf Ericson school and I really enjoyed it.

Diane also stayed in San Diego at the same time, so on the weekends she would pick me up and we'd go and hang together. We never got to Sea World, but she promised me that we would sometimes. I enjoyed going

on the weekends with Diane because Auntie Jean became too religious.

Dwayne, her son was bad. He carved a cross on my leg with a razor blade. When the teacher asked what had happened, I told her the truth. The teacher called Auntie Jean and she blamed me and wanted to whoop me for lying. She asked Dwayne if he did it and he told the truth about it. Auntie beat the living crap out of him.

Her daughter Da Wanna also didn't like me. They had a skylight in the ceiling and because I loved to look up at the stars, they thought I worshiped the devil. I was accused of all sorts of things because of this. Auntie Jean would also make me sit at the table to eat all my vegetables just like Papa would do. I'd spit it out into a napkin, and once, I put it in the clothes hamper by mistake, I was caught and got a whooping for it,

Auntie Jean had a little stand/alter on her table in the dining room. She'd always have a plate placed on it with fruit on the side with a big glass of water and she'd tell me not to touch it because it was for Jesus. This was her way to welcome Jesus in. I would run down the steps late at night to see if Jesus would come.

One night, I took a little off the plate to make Auntie feel better because Jesus never did come. Of course, she got upset with me, but I didn't get a whooping for that because she knew I was trying to make her feel better.

I would say, "Jesus came right? He liked your cooking and he came."

Da Wanna was sitting at the top of the steps one night and I was watching TV. Da Wanna fell down the stairs and she told her mother that I was the devil-possessed and I caused her to fall. She believed her, and because of this and the cross and other incidents, I was sent back home.

I remember one year, we didn't have too much money, Papa was mad at me so I went to Momma and she gave me about $25.00 which was good for only one day at a carnival that was in town. After tickets, and games, and stuff, everything was so high. I'd taken someone with me so, I ended up just splurging money that I didn't have, and I spent it all in one day.

I wanted to go the next day of course so, that night I reached my hand inside a little cabinet where there was a music box and I knew they use to keep money in there but what I didn't know was that it was the church's money. Anyway, I got it and went to the carnival the next day and that Sunday when they got ready to get the money, it wasn't there. Of course, they knew that I had gotten it. I got the worst beating of my life and Momma had to replace the money. I don't think the church ever found out because they replaced it.

Around this same time, De Shane's mother would come to visit her. She didn't like me and it was mutual. One thing about De Shane is that she was scary and the timid type back then. We never saw eye to eye and I think that's why her mother didn't' care for me. When she was in the 3rd of 4th grade at age 8 or 9, one of her classmates wanted to beat her up. I jumped in to defend her as a

good big sister would, but even with that, she still didn't like me. The only time we got along was when we'd go over to Aunt Dot's and play with Winnie.

Papa noticed me and Winnie playing with her Easy-Bake-Oven one day, so on my last Christmas there, he got me one of my own. He'd still let me have anything I wanted even though he also was still whooping my ass for anything and everything. The only problem with the oven was that sometimes Papa would have 1 fan plugged in so he said we couldn't plug anything else in because we had to save on electricity.

Sometimes, I don't know how we stayed cool cause Papa always had the one fan turned on him alone, and the other fan stayed in the closet, and we couldn't touch it.

One day Papa was in bed, and we were in the living room. I went in the closet to get the big fan out. It was in a box. I put it right inside the window by Papa's chair, the window was just the right size and so big that we could all feel the nice cool air. The next morning Papa asked,

"Who put the fan in the window?"

"I did it," I said.

"You know better than that." He replied.

And I thought I was going to get it again so I had to come up with something quick. I said,

"You weren't getting enough air from that little fan Papa. This big fan will cool everyone off, and it's still pointing at you."

He liked that idea. I learned a good lesson that day, that was how to manipulate Papa and get him to agree with me.

Now Marvilyn was different from De Shane. She gave me my first cigarette, and we'd smoke out the bedroom window or smoke across the fence outside. My friend Charmaine who stayed across the street and I would go over to Marvilyn's and get her weed and smoke it up. Marvilyn paid for other stuff with her weed which I didn't know at the time. But we still would hang together sometimes.

I remember when her son Shawn was 5 years old, he stole $400.00 from Momma and he went to the corner store and was giving it away and spending it up. His stepfather Daryl came and found him with it, but they blamed me for it. I have no idea why.

Edward Gardner and Mattie White Rented the apartment upstairs when it was empty again. They had four children, their sons; Casey, Reginald, Oshea, and Tonya their daughter. Casey was the oldest child. He grew up with me because he was closest to my age. I may have been a year older than he was. They came from Little Rock, AK.

In the back yard, we had a swing set with a slide and they use to play on the set with us. We 'd act like we were boxing and play hide and seek and stuff like that. We

were always together because we all lived in the same house. Tonya was too young, but De Shane and I would play with them. Also, Willene Moss would join in some times because she stayed with her parents Carrie and Nathanial Moss downstairs in the basement apartment.

Casey got a skateboard when they first came out. It was weird because they didn't celebrate Christmas because they were Muslim. What made it so bad, is that Mattie didn't want me to ride on it. But one day, I took it when Casey wasn't there. They saw me down the street on the skateboard from out the window, Edward chased me down the street but he didn't catch me. I threw it under the car to hide it just in time, and it didn't break.

When they asked me about it, I denied that I'd had it, and I didn't take it back. Instead, I lied and said It wasn't me that they saw riding it. It was nice too, with precision wheels. I didn't' feel bad about it either because I couldn't understand why they wouldn't let me ride it in the first place. Casey and them were able to share my swing set. They'd play tag, hide and seek, catch can with me. Why couldn't I play with their things?

There were good times to be had at the Hancox house too. Sometimes because I remember so much of the bad, I forget about the good things. Like, I got all kinds of toys that last Christmas along with my Easy-Bake-Oven. I got food to go with it, as well as baby dolls with clothes for them to wear, and I got a lot of Barbie Dolls too. De Shane got a new Snow Cone maker and the Baby-That-Away that crawled around. We both were happy because

she made snow cones and I made cakes. We played with those toys all year, even during the summer.

One summer day, I hung a sign out that said "Cakes and Snow Cones" and we got 3 people to come by. But they found out that the cakes came from my easy-bake-oven, so they looked sad because it wasn't one of Momma's home-made cakes.

Momma used to make all kinds of home-made cakes, pies, peach cobbler, and her famous home-made ice cream and tea cakes. She made cakes for the church and us. We all liked to lick the batter out of the bowl and off the spoon after she poured it into the pans. There was nothing like tasting that cake batter that she left in the bowl for us kids to taste. Papa always got the first piece of anything she made.

We use to go to Stoney island which was a street on the east side of Chicago. The place was called Fun-Town and it was like an amusement park open all year round. It had a couple of roller coasters for us kids and it was a place I loved to go to. Momma didn't like the area that it was in, but I didn't see any difference.

I remember one time when I couldn't get on the roller-coaster ride.

"Hey, Mom. Momma, Momma, come over here. Oh, I love Cotton Candy. Would you buy me some Cotton Candy please?"

"Okay, I'll get you some Cotton Candy."

"Momma?"

"Yes Baby, now get in line."

"Oh, I love to ride the roller-coasters, Can I ride that one? Please, please? Oh, I like that one, that one goes really really fast,"

"Here's your Cotton-Candy baby."

"Oh, thank you, Mom,"

Momma and I would walk over to the roller-coaster ride and stand and wait for the man to let me on. He would say,

"Oh no, she's too small for this one. She has to go over there. She's not tall enough for this ride."

"Oh Momma, please make him let me get on, please make him Momma, please?"

"I'm sorry Ruth, you can't get on. You're just a little bit too short. Next time I'll let you wear some heels so you can pass." She said smiling.

"Oh, Mom, I wanna get on so bad. It goes so, so fast."

"Well you don't' need to get on that one anyway, I'm scared for you to get on that one it goes too fast. Anything could happen."

"Oh, Mom. Now I have to go over here with the little kiddies."

"Oh Ruth, it'll still be fun."

"Alright. Let's go over here to this one then. It's the Zipper, and you get locked in a cage and I know this one's fun Mom. I hope I can ride this one, I hope so much."

We move over to the Zipper with me chewing on my Cotton Candy.

"Oh, I passed, I passed. It'll be so much fun, Momma."

"Hey little girl," the man said, "You cannot take that Cotton Candy with you."

"You mean I have to throw my Candy away?"

"Yes sweetheart, you have to throw it away before getting on the ride,"

"Oh, no. Momma, Momma come back. Here Momma, hold my Cotton Candy for me."

I'd get on the ride and shout, "Oh No! It's going too fast. Stop, Stop." Then I'd get off the ride and throw up everywhere. Next thing you know,

"Momma, Momma, can I get a Candy Apple? Please, Please?" And Papa would say,

"You gave her too much candy and too many sweets. She's already done threw up, she really don't need nothing else. She's too damn spoiled as it is."

"Oh Papa," Momma would say back, "This is why we come so that they can eat Cotton Candy and Candied Apples. Would you like one?"

"Hm, yeah I think I'll take a Candy Apple myself."

"Okay, well we'll get in line and get 2 Candy Apples."

And we'd go to ride after ride and it was so much fun with me and Momma and Papa spending all day together.

We'd also go to Old Chicago which was another amusement park. It closed down, but it was like Great America or Six-Flags, only it was indoors. It was huge with the same type of roller coasters and everything. A couple of kids got hurt eventually so it did shut down. Upstairs was a mall with stores. I would go in the stores and steal a few of those huge lollipops, then I'd go back downstairs and ride on the huge rides.

Every time I went to old Chicago, I would manage to steal a couple of lollipops. It didn't take much. I'd take them out of the candy holders than pretend to look around, and then walk out the stores with 'em. I never got caught. It was great.

Then there was Great America in Chicago. I never got sick on the roller coaster rides and I liked the biggest ones that would go upside down. I just couldn't ride the Ferris Wheels or the Merry-Go-Round, or anything that circled around like the swings. I would get sick on those types of rides. But the ones that went upside down and over and under, just like my life, I would love to ride on those.

WHY DIDN'T YOU KNOW?   by: Ruth Hancox

Well, back to the bad, once again. One day, I talked back
to Papa and kind of rolled my eyes and smacked my lips.
He immediately ran into his room and got his revolver
out and my mother ran in the living room and told me to
ran for my life. I ran down 111th street like a wild child
because somebody was trying to kill me. Then after that
Momma jumped in her car and went searching for me.

I hid by Bell Lumber company where there was a lot of
wood and lumber laying around. While I was hiding
there, I saw that big, green, 69 Cadillac coming down the
street and I knew it was Momma coming to rescue me.
She got me and took me to Aunt Dot's house.

I was able to play with Winnie, but that night, Ricochet,
oh my God here we go again. Everyone was asleep so he
took me to his bed that night and had sex with me all
night long and Ricochet was really, really big down there
so it hurt a whole lot. When he was supposed to go to
school the next day, He wouldn't let me out of the room
because everyone else was up. He made me jump out the
window which was upstairs, and jump off the roof. Then
he came and opened the door. That was so stupid, and
dangerous.

Chapter Six: The Big Lie, Then Leaving the Hancox House

Ephesians 6 – 4: and ye fathers provoke not your children to wrath but bring them up in the nurture and admonition of the lord

One night De Shane and I were in the room getting ready for bed. Momma would always give us money so we could go to the store. I would save all my candy up until night time and De Shane would eat all of her candy during the day. So, this night, when I got ready to eat my candy, it was gone. I turned to De Shane,

"What happened to all my candy Shane?"

"I don't know?"

"That's some bullshit, you ate all my candy, didn't you?"

"I wouldn't do that. I had my own candy."

"But you already ate yours this afternoon. I know you ate my candy, Shane. Nobody else is here. You know, it's time you got a real ass whooping from me. I'm so tired of your bullshit it ain't even funny."

But before I could grab her, she ran into the living room where Papa was.

"Papa, Papa, Ruth said she's gonna kick my ass for no good reason. She just said she was tired of me and that I needed a good ass whooping. For no reason Papa."

"What?" Papa said. "So, you're tired of you sister huh," he said as he came and stood in front of me, "Well I'm sick and tired of your shit."

Wham!

He hit me right in the face. Blood started shooting out of my nose instantly and I fell to the floor. When I got up, he hit me again, "Wham" and knocked me back down. I got up again and he did it again. I didn't know that I was supposed to stay down. After the 3rd time, I came up with the bar stool which was sitting right there next to me. I hit him "BAM", and ran out of the house. I didn't know that I had knocked his pacemaker out of place.

When I came to my senses, I turned around and tried to go back, but they wouldn't let me in. They held the door closed in my face. When they were so carried away with keeping me out, I knew that it was serious. I realized

what I'd done and I tried to go to him but they thought I wanted to continue the fight.

I waited outside for a little bit while they were waiting for the ambulance to come. His heart was acting up and the family believed that if I came back into the house, Papa may get too upset and die. I was never allowed to return to the house. Little did they know that this incident would change my whole life forever.

I had to start staying with other people after that; I had to leave home for good. One of the first friends I went to for help, who lived up the street, was Rochelle. But Rochelle's mother told her to stop playing with me. Her mother told her that I killed my father. They thought Papa had died. I was 11 years old.

Tony was a pimp, and Cynthia was his girlfriend and the mother of his children. I moved in with them because she was Marvilyn's sister, and theirs was the only place I knew I could go to at my age after I was kicked out of the Hancox house. Tony had 3 or 4 girls working for him at the time I moved in. One was named Dawn. We use to sleep in the same bed together along with Susan.

Tony started by taking pictures of me in the nude and he'd sell them to his friends, his fellow band members, and also to just people on the street. He's the one who got me started in prostitution. He'd dress all of us girls up in big boots and long wigs and tell us to go to work.

After my 12th birthday, I had to stand on the corner at my young age and I didn't know what to do, but I had to

make money or else he would beat me half to death along with anyone else who didn't make the cut. How he did it was, he would wait till we got in the tub, then he'd take a wire clothes hanger and wrap it up with a handkerchief. Then he'd beat us up with it.

Cynthia, his so-called wife, would have nervous breakdowns every once in a while, and would go to the hospital. She did this for years, and sometimes she would just run away for days at a time. But she had kids by him so he had a little compassion for her and wouldn't be as bad to her as he was to the rest of us, including Gigi, Cynthia's cousin, who tried to get in the band as a singer. Most of the time Cynthia would trick him and make him think she had a breakdown just to get away from him.

I was kind of glad going into prostitution because in my mind, I mine as well sell it, then to let them take it. So that's when I started being a professional prostitute. I had good days and bad. I wanted to make it a career because it was easy money. A few Johns did take it, but I can't call it rape because it was just bad decision making on my part. I didn't get my money upfront, and I didn't go with my gut instincts by being more careful. Tony had taught us that if we were going to be a prostitute, we had to be a good one by getting the money upfront every time.

After a while living with Cynthia and Tony became too much for me. Tony taught us little things about street life, and I was able to get along, but I was so tired of living like that. So, I ended up turning myself into the police. I was considered a runaway because I was still young and had left the Hancox home. The police were still looking

for me at the time. I went back with them to 111th street where they called children's services who came and got me and put me in a juvenile detention center.

I stayed there for about 6 months which was on 11th and Hamilton in Chicago. Momma and Papa came to let them know that they didn't want me back in their home and they wanted to take their name Hancox back. They didn't want anything more to do with me. Momma told them this when we went to court and made sure that the judge knew that she didn't want me back. It destroyed me, but there was nothing that I could do about it. The court security guard took me back upstairs and I had to ride that bus back to the juvenile detention center.

They found another foster home for me because I was too big for an orphanage. Some of the kids in the Juvenile Detention Center were there only because they couldn't find a place to put them, which was so cruel. But I was placed in a foster home shortly after arriving there.

The foster mother was trying to get me to talk, and I couldn't. I just looked at her and refused to talk. It was close to the Roseland area and Calumet city. I just didn't understand why they wanted to talk to me. I remember getting a bedroom of my own and everything, but I didn't want to stay there. I didn't know what to do, and it was the first time I remember being a foster kid. I was a baby when I was given to the Hancox', and I didn't remember any of it. I didn't know anything about this type of l life. I didn't know what these people wanted from me, so I sat on the side of the bed for days.

They wanted me to go to a school that was so far away and yet, they didn't give me any money to get there. I had to walk, and I got tired of it. Sometimes, I would walk there but I wouldn't go inside the building once I got there. I didn't know which buses to take back home, and no one explained it to me, so I'd walk. It was so tiring that I'd skip school because I didn't want to walk anymore.

Eventually, I did figure out how to catch the city bus, but it took forever and I still didn't get money for it, so I started panhandling to get the money. I had already started smoking so instead of catching the bus, I'd get cigarettes. I also knew how to smoke weed. I'd buy bags of weed with the money. There was nothing wrong with the house or anything, I just didn't know what to do for the new foster parents. They thought I'd been in foster care before but they didn't know that it was when I was a baby and too young to know anything.

One day I got fed up, so I walked to the Hancox house from my new foster home. I wanted to apologize and come back home. When Momma came to the door, she said that Papa had passed. I was devastated. I felt so bad that I didn't get to apologize to him. She wouldn't even let me in the house because she said that Papa wouldn't have wanted that. So, I left feeling so lonely and abandoned.

A couple of days later I went back, and Momma told me when the funeral was. I didn't get to ride in the front car with the family because they wouldn't let me, but I got there just in time to march in the processional. Momma said she knew I'd be there, and of course; I was. But everybody treated me so cold, and so mean, they didn't

want me around. All his kids Maurice, Larry, June-bug, the Mosses, none of them wanted me at that funeral or the house afterward.

During the funeral, Momma screamed out so loud, like she was releasing him in his death. When I heard it, it went through me with such an Icey coldness, I too was released with her scream. Released from all that guilt caused by Papa. I went out and lived a whole different life after that.

He actually died of pneumonia, not because of his pacemaker being knocked off. Six months later after getting out of the hospital once his pacemaker was fixed, he lived a normal life but he'd go outside without a hat on and stuff like that, and that was the cause of his death.

There was a blizzard the day of the funeral, so I stayed at the church afterward. They were having some type of 4-H meeting there so I participated, then I walked back to the Hancox house. The whole family was sitting in the Livingroom as I rang the doorbell. They let me in, so I sat in the corner for about 4 hours without talking to anybody.

I went to the other room to talk to Diane, she acknowledged and hugged me, but nobody else would even talk to me, so I went to talk to my Momma. When the family saw this, they all came in and told me not to talk to her, but Momma hugged me and told me,

"Don't let nobody tell you that you killed your father."

I wanted to stay the night because of the blizzard but they wouldn't let me, so I went back to the church for a while. I knew a way to get back inside without anyone knowing, so, I snuck into the church where Papa's body was still on display. I talked to Papa all night long.

After the funeral and papa's burial and everything was over, I went back to the foster home and the lady had called my caseworker and told her I could no longer stay with her because I had stayed away so long without calling her. I didn't even have her phone number and didn't even know the people's names to tell you the truth.

They took me to 2020 Roosevelt road. I entered the building for my intake and sat in the lobby waiting for the paperwork to be done. They forgot I was there. They were waiting for a placement for me to come in but they never found one. I went into the building on a Thursday, but they left me there. I was there all-day Friday, Saturday, and Sunday and they didn't' know it. Monday came and I was still sitting there. I think that I had gone into shock because I didn't talk, I didn't eat, so, they ended up taking me to Ravenswood hospital and I stayed there for about 2 months without talking. They had to put a tube in me so I could eat.

They waited to see if I was going to come around and respond. After I started responding, they took out the tube and gave me Jell-O and ice cream. There was this nurse who would come to talk to me every Friday and read the bible telling me that I was too young to waste away like this. The part of Ravenswood that I was in was the mental institution ward.

They then moved me to the hospital part when they saw that they could feed me through the tube. My mother sent some of my clothes through the caseworker which the caseworker stole half of those. After I left Ravenswood, I ended up at Ms. Thurman's house. She was pretty nice, and she had a daughter named Betty, and Betty's boyfriend was named Alonzo.

A friend that I went to school with, Cidel, would come over and bring me big bags of candy. And my 6th-grade teacher, Ms. Foyer, who failed everyone in the class, brought over some certificates which I'd gotten while attending school. I had gotten it in math but she still failed the whole class in every other subject but math. Just before she failed everyone, I had switched to another school so I didn't get failed. I got to go into the next grade even though I didn't know what they were doing.

Ms. Thurman would have fun with drinking and partying. She'd let me ride an old bike which was in the basement while I was there, and I had a friend named Sherri and two more foster kid stayed there as well. We would sit on the front porch and smoke weed and have fun with all the other fosters in the house. But Sherri would like to grind all night long and I got sick of that shit and told on her. She was worse than a Nigga. So, they moved me downstairs and out of that room, away from her. And made her stop.

I started getting bad and mischievous out of boredom. Ms. Thurman's husband would be drunk all the time and try to touch on me too, but I got him back really good. One night he got so drunk that I was able to get up under

his pillow and get $500.00 of his. I went back towards Ada park and bought all my friends something good with that money, and we smoked weed all night long. I went back to the house and they thought Sherri had done it, so I just went along with that and got off scot-free.

Eventually, they ended up moving me and all the other children out and I think it was because Ms. Thurman got sick. So, I ended up going into a group home. And this time, I didn't like it, so I ran away. When they caught me, the caseworker ended up sending me to Quincy, Il so I wouldn't run away again. It was nice, big, and pretty but it was the worse group home I ever went to.

There was this girl named Polar who was much older than me, and Amy, a white girl who was always waking me up in the middle of the night and hunching me. At night we'd sneak down the fire escape and go to the liquor store on the corner and we'd get drunk.

We'd be in this dorm along with so many women, and we'd be sick and smelling like liquor. But no one ever chastised us because there were just too many girls there. All we did was get drunk all the time. We'd never go to school or anything. That's all we did for at least a year.

We did go once to an amusement park and they had to force me back in the van to go back. I wanted to stay and work there maybe help clean it or something. So, when I got back, I started a fire in the basement. There were 4 of us that use to hang together all the time. They knew it had to be one of us 4. So, they transferred us to another

juvenile detention center and we were locked into our rooms, which was right next to a cemetery.

I just knew that I was gonna die or something bad was going to happen to me there. Eventually, they let me out and the caseworker was there. They put me back on a plane, back to Chicago, back to another locked facility called Essex Detention Center on the east side of Chicago. They take away all your clothes and you are in pajamas all the time. It was a locked setting. You're in Pjs for about a month, then you can go to school.

Somehow all of us managed to smoke cigarettes. Doris and Mable were there with me, and they showed me the ropes about how to go across the street and steal cigarettes and never go back to school. Doris and I tied up the staff, got the petty cash, and then left. I never saw that place again.

We slept in the garage of the Hancox for about a month, then stayed with Marvilyn for a little while. They never blamed me for tying up the staff, Doris may have taken the blame for that, I don't know. So, it all ended up with me going to The Herrick House in Cook County, IL, which was where they shot the movie, Jason. I liked it there somewhat. There was this staff named Clarissa and I loved her, Emit, and Donna. They would bring me stuff from home and bring it to my room. I was the youngest one there and it was nice. The whole setting was nice.

They would give us an allowance for doing chores and I'd save it up for a few months. We were far away from society in the woods. I would have to catch a train back to

Chicago when Marvilyn would let me go there to visit her for the weekends.

Eventually, I ended up at a hospital called the Reed Zone. The Reed Zone was a hospital for children where I met this guy named Jerry Reed. He was my age and his mother used to beat on him and that's how he ended up at the hospital

He was on the boy's side and I was on the girl's side. We use to have dances at the Reed Zone and that was the opportunity for us to socialize together. Jerry and I use to talk and sit down together, and he always had money so he'd buy me hot dogs, and popcorn, and sodas, and stuff. He was a nice guy but I didn't really like him like as a boyfriend, I use to just like him because he was a nice guy.

He was like,

"Let's get outta here."

We found out we were from the same neighborhood so we would sneak out. There was this tall fence with barbed wire at the top cause we were locked into this institution. They would leave the door open on the side for the older kids to step out and have a cigarette while at the dance. But once it got dark, they would close the door. This particular time, they forgot to close the door so as we stepped out, it was dark still so we headed for the woods and ran into this big tall fence with barbed wire. We climbed the fence and jumped over the wire, and we ran for our lives.

We ran until we found the bus line, and we got on the bus and ended up back on 111th street and Marvilyn lived in the back still. So, we went back there where she was to ask if we could stay. Before he left Reed Zone, Jerry had stolen a pair of diamond earrings from one of the workers which he gave to me. They were real diamonds too. 3-carat diamond earrings and I ended up giving them to Marvilyn because she liked them. I didn't really know the value but she did, so, I gave them to her. I asked if she could let me and Jerry stay and she did. She let us stay for a little while.

Chapter Seven: Back Home Again – My Husband

Proverbs 20 – 1: wine is a mocker strong drink is raging and whosoever is deceived thereby is not wise.

My sister Marvilyn lived in the house behind Momma's house with Daryl Wilson, her boyfriend. The house was originally built by Papa for his son Uncle Quinn. She invited me to stay with her when I finally came out of the system.

I was welcomed back home to spend time with Aisha who was about 4 yrs. old, Marvilyn's daughter, and Shawn's sister. She was born and I was so happy that once again, I had someone I could take care of. I would dress her up and take her to the church and the park. I would tell everyone that she was my baby but they knew she wasn't. By this time, I was receiving Papa's Social Security check and I would go shopping to get her all sorts of things.

Before this, she had told Momma not to let me come back home. She said I'd destroy her, I'd destroy everything, I wasn't worth nothing, I'm good for nothing, but Momma wouldn't listen so she let me come back home and Jerry stood there like my brother but she really couldn't keep him too so she called his caseworker and got permission for him to live with us. So, he stayed in Momma's house for a long time even after Earl came.

Upstairs, also in Momma's house, lived a man named Rayford who lived there with his wife Jeanette who was a nurse. Rayford and Marvilyn showed me how to free-base Cocaine.

I had been saving my allowance for weeks and I had about $700.00 on me. Marvilyn and Rayford talked me into buying it and then showed me how to cook it and smoke it.

They were both there that first day. As soon as I came into her house, Marvilyn said,

"Girl, I know you got some money. Give me some money."

"For what?" I said, "What you need some money for Marvilyn?"

"Girl, shit, so we can get high."

"High? Off of what?"

"Off Cocaine."

"Cocaine? What the hell is Cocaine?"

"Shit girl," Marvilyn said laughing, looking at Rayford, "you'll find out. Come on Bitch, let me show you what we gonna do."

"Alright Hoe, come on." I threw back, giving her $50.00 the first time.

She goes and buys it. Comes back and says,

"Sit your ass down here in this chair. Let me show you how to cook this shit up."

"Okay."

She mixed it with baking soda, then put it in a test tube, puts water in it and places it over the fire from the burner on the gas stove. She shakes it around while it's heating up. After the powder turns into a liquid, she takes it off the stove, puts some cold water in it, and then grabs a bent-up wire clothes hanger saying,

"Now watch this shit."

She squeezes the bent clothes hanger down inside the test tube as I'm looking at it, and stirs the Cocaine and water up together. As she's stirring it up, it's getting hard and clinging to the clothes hanger. Then she pulls out the hanger with the hardened Cocaine wrapped around its tip. Then she says,

"Now bitch, watch what I'm doing. Pay God-damned attention 'cause you're not supposed to hit the sides. Don't

hit the sides. Don't let it rub on the side of the glass. Cause you'll be leaving your Cocaine in there."

"Oh, okay."

She took the hanger, spread the Cocaine on the mirror. She put a spoon on it and rubbed the spoon all in it. I asked her,

"What's that for?"

"That's how you dry it."

"Dry it?"

"Yes bitch, dry it."

After she got it dried and all on the mirror, she took it and she scraped it up with a razor blade and it came back in powdered form just the way it was when she put it in there. I couldn't understand why she went through all that just to have it come out the same way. I was like,

"Hell Nah... how you do that? You a killer full of magic tricks."

She said, "Nah, you'll see the magic, wait till you hit this shit."

I was like, "Okay."

So, her and Rayford hit first, then she gave the pipe to me. They put some of the new powder on the pipe for me, and she said,

"Pull off of it. Now push it to your head, hold onto it and push it to your head. Don't let it go. Then blow it out slowly."

And I did. And I was very happy. I was like,

"Did I do it right? Did I do it right?"

"Well you gotta do it a few more times so you can get it just right."

So, she grabbed the next package. Then she said,

"Now, I need for you to come over here and try to cook some of this shit up."

So, I tried it. When I was over the fire my hands got to shaking, and she took my hands and was guiding me, and she kept telling me,

"Girl, stop being so fucking nervous, the shit is not going to burn you. You can't let it get that fucking hot so, don't get nervous."

I was like, "Okay."

After the first time, it was never quite the same again. My drug use progressed and I kept doing it. I was only about 13 at the time.

One day Momma saw me in her back yard and invited me to come back home, but De Shane didn't want me to go back, so Momma withdrew her offer. She took De Shane's side because they always thought that I was bad,

getting into a lot of fights, and I would come home with black eyes and stuff like that. I remember when a guy named Rollo raped me. He was an ugly skinny black man who wore a cap all the time. He Smelled like alcohol and Wild Irish Rose wine and would talk constantly. He had a hard-right hook and he ended up giving me a black eye.

I was riding my bike at Ada park and he came out of nowhere and snatched me off the bike. He dragged me to this house and threw me inside I backed away from him against the wall. Nobody saw what happened so I knew I was in trouble.

"Bitch, come here. You gonna be my Hoe tonight." He said. "Shit, I'm a put this dick in you. Now get on this dick and suck this dick. Let me show you something. Let me show you what it's all about.

He had grabbed me and put his dick out for me to suck on it. I had no choice but to do it. He talked the whole time.

"You like this dick? You like this big black dick? Now lick on them balls. Bitch, you bet-not stop."

During this, he continued to hit me in my face and the back of my head. I kept hollering,

"Stop! Stop! I'll do it! I'll do it! I'll suck it!"

"Now turn around, and let me get that booty hole."

Then he fucked me in my ass. Oh, God. I don't think I can even explain how bad it was. I came home with that black

eye, and all those bruises and nobody even seemed to see it.

I told one person about it; her name was Judy Dickerson. I went to church that Sunday and was singing in the choir and crying. She noticed and came over to ask me what had happened. I couldn't' tell her right then, but then I saw him coming from rehearsal and I called her and told her everything. She came over to the house and confronted my mother. She asked her how could she miss that gigantic black eye that I had? Do you know what my mother said? "It was a figment of her imagination". Are you shittin' me? After that, I couldn't tell Momma anything.

I continued to live with Marvilyn. I played in Momma's backyard a lot. I'd run around trying to get back to a normal life, little did I know that my future husband was watching me from Marvilyn's window. He was around 26 and way too old for me. I should have known then that Marvilyn didn't really love me, she introduced me to him, and free-basing Cocaine.

How we met was, I was playing in the water hole in the backyard. Irving came outside and began to talk to me.

"Hey there, little Sugar. You look so cute. I haven't seen you around here before, what's your name?"

"Ruth. I'm Marvilyn's sister."

"Really? I remember her talking about a sister named Ruth, but she never said how adorable you are. I'm a friend of hers, my names Irving, but everybody calls me Earl. Would you like to call me Earl?"

"Okay," I said blushing. He was kind a cute too.

"It's been a long time since I've seen someone as pretty as you. You'd look gorgeous on my arm if you'd allow me to escort you out to dinner. Would you like that?"

"Dinner? You wanna take me out to dinner?"

"Yes, I do. How 'bout it?"

"Okay. But I have to change clothes."

"That would be wonderful. I'll meet you here at 6:00 tonight. Okay?"

"I'll be here."

"All right now, until then, you fine lil sugar. See you later."

I watched him walk away and back into my sister's house. I couldn't believe. He actually wanted to take me out to a fancy restaurant to have dinner. I couldn't wait. Later on, that evening I got dressed, and that night, I went out to dinner with him I was 13 years old.

I thought that I looked really good for him. We had a really good dinner and after that, he'd come over every day and he would bring me chocolates, or one long stem rose, or a dozen roses. And this went on for some time.

We began to smoke weed together outside or in Marvilyn's house. And one night he came over and said that he could not get back home and he asked can he spend the night. I asked my Momma and she said yes. I was living back with her at the time. She never objected about him coming over even as old as he was. She never said anything about him being too old, she did ask me once if I was happy and I said yes.

He was in Johnny's old room, and I was in mine. I acted like I was asleep; I knew he would come to the room and he did. He made it down the hallway, made it into the room and climbed into my bed and I was already ready for him, I didn't have on any panties but I still acted like was sleep with my legs wide open.

"Oh, my sweet Sugar. Look at you, all ready for me like this. You look so soft and tasty."

So, he started caressing me and touching my body really soft using his fingers to get me ready. I was loving every minute of it.

"So wet and juicy for me. I can't wait to taste my sweet chocolate sugar. You want me, babe? You want what I have for you? I can tell you want it. I know you ain't sleeping, let me see your eyes baby."

I was really enjoying him. It was no longer rape, it was love. He made love to me all night and I still acted like I was sleep.

He whispered in my ear, "I know you're not asleep, please move your body around."

I started laughing so loud, that Momma woke up. She called my name so; he ran back into his room.

After that we were like tick and tack when you saw him, you saw me. We started out smoking weed, then we went to pills, then free-basing Cocaine. After 3 years together, he asked me to marry him.

When I was going to school in the 6th grade, I met this boy. He also asked me to marry him around the same time. I remember that my choice was between him and my husband, and I ended up picking my husband because he was older and more mature. This guy had money, a car, and a business. But I ended up picking a loser. Eddie was his name; he was truly in love with me. On some occasions later, when my husband would go to jail, he would come over to see me and make sure I had some money in my pocket and stuff like that.

We wanted to get married by Reverend Meeks who was Momma's pastor, but he refused to marry us at the church that I grew up in, so we asked another Reverend named Moore. We got married in Momma's house, and even though there wasn't a lot of people there, the people I liked were there and his Grandfather was also there.

We spent our honeymoon in the back room of my
Mommas house spending 3 weeks with wine, beer,
cocaine, and pills. We had every type of pipe you can
imagine that you can smoke out of. Momma brought food
and made sure that we ate. She'd bring the food to the
room, and this lasted for 3 weeks.

After coming out of the room Momma had prepared the
apartment downstairs for us to move into and had it all
cleaned up with new linen and we moved downstairs.
Earl would fix on cars; he was a good mechanic.
Everyone in the neighborhood called him, that's how he
would make extra money and Momma would take care of
the rest. We didn't want for anything. He also had his side
hustle which was stealing cars.

My friend Jerry from the Reed Zone and Earl never got
along because I think Jerry was really in love with me
and he wouldn't let anything happen to me, He always
protected me and wouldn't let anybody try to fight me. If
anyone got in my face, he would fight for me. So, I didn't
have anything to worry about as long as Jerry was
around. But, after Earl and I got married, he left and I
hated that he left, but he would still come to visit every
once in a while. But when he did, he and Earl would get
into it.

We use to play cards all the time with people in the
neighborhood. We would have spade tournaments and
we'd sit around and drink some E & J Brandy and
whoever would lose would have to chug it all down at
one time, we were buying it by the gallon.

And we'd do what's called scherm sticks and we were doing tack, it's like powder. We'd just do every type of pills or drugs that there was to do. Everyone would come over to our house which was considered the spot, and we'd sell weed. Earl taught me how to bag up the weed and sell it. We always had money in our pockets which helped my Mom because she didn't have to support our habits.

We did this for a long time until somebody got mad and told the police on us. One day we came home and my Mom was gone to bible study but there was something strange about the house. I had a strange feeling and I knew something was wrong because all the lights were turned out and my Mom never did that.

I told Earl to drive around the block a couple of times and I couldn't figure out what was wrong but I knew that it was something strange and I had that feeling. But we were so frantic to get back into the house to get high so we pulled into the driveway. We didn't see anyone, no police or anything. So, we went into the house and into the basement where we stayed. We started cooking up the cocaine and about 10 minutes later, we heard a boom. That was the police coming in the front door.

They were already in the house, in my Moms part of the house. My Momma never left without leaving the kitchen light on. I should have known that they were there because that kitchen light was always on so that you could see inside the house from the outside and it was out that night. She had even told us that if that kitchen light was ever out, something was wrong. But I had forgotten

what she told me because I was too busy trying to get high.

They ended up taking Earl to jail but there really was not enough evidence to get me because we had already done all the cocaine, there was only a little bit left on the mirror by the time we heard the boom and when I heard it, I jumped and the mirror flew up in the air and we had stepped in it and trampled it down into the floor.

That was the day we couldn't find any weed either so there wasn't anything in the house to convict us of any major crime. What I didn't know at the time was that we could have sued the police department because they didn't have any type of warrant and they kicked in my mother's door unannounced. That just shows you how when you don't know anything about the law, the police could just run over you and get away with it.

Chapter Eight: Crime, Passion and Pain

My husband taught me how to steal cars. Anything with a tilt on it I knew how to steal. Especially sports cars, Trans-Ams and Corvettes and anything with a tee top. The tee tops went for $250.00 and back then it was good money. We'd take the cars to the chop shops and get $500.00 for them.

A few times the police got after us with some high-speed chases, but we got away every time. I had a 69 Cadillac which was Momma's but she no longer drove it so, either I or Earl would drive it. I didn't know I had to have a driver's license to drive. Momma would just give me the keys and tell me to drive it. Earl taught me how to dodge the police.

One thing I'd do for fun during those times would be to get in the car and drive down to go visit Diane with Earl. We use to go visit her all the time when she was smoking weed. We would smoke weed together and have a good time. She was always like a good sister to me, I loved going to see her and stuff like that.

But back home, Earl and I were stealing cars and smoking dope all the time and we were on Cocaine really bad. He went to jail and so I had to prostitute again but then Momma would give me money also so I wouldn't have to walk the streets at night. This went on for some time.

WHY DIDN'T YOU KNOW?   by: Ruth Hancox

Curtis Mitchell grew up with me. I knew him before I knew my husband. Now Curtis was one of the boys who never did rape me, I use to give it to him in back of the van sometimes or over to his house. I use to sit and talk to his mother on her porch a lot and she knew that I liked her son. When I was about 6 or 7 years old, she used to talk to me all the time. I just loved her, and use to pretend that I was her daughter. But as we got older and I got married, Curtis used to come over to play cards with us. But then, something happened between him and my husband.

At the time Earl and I use to sell weight, and we would carry all types of guns. I had a dowager and we had an Uzi with a banana clip. Somehow Curtis and my husband got into it and we went down 111th place and I was just shooting out the car. And before the crew broke up, we use to always drink and get high and then we'd go in the Jewish grand bazar store and I'd pretend like I was having a seizure and they'd go in the back and steal some liquor. To me, that was some of the fun days.

We would drive out in the 69 Cadillac that Momma would let me drive. We'd go out to the cemetery and drink and smoke. Someone would always have to get out to go pee and we'd take off. We would always come back and get them but it was funny leaving them there for a few minutes thinking we had left them behind. We use to walk through the cemetery as kids and scare each other.

I got pregnant with my first son at 17 years old and once I got pregnant, seemed like Earl changed. His love was

dying down. I was growing up and I felt like his love had changed but I was so dumb.

One day while I was pregnant, he drove to a friend's house which I found out was his girlfriend. She was just as pregnant as I was. He stayed in the house with her for 3 to 4 hours and I was sitting outside in that hot car. So, I got to cursing and I knocked on the door and her brother answered and showed me back to the girl's room where she was with him. I stormed back to the car but still had to wait because he had the keys. So, I waited till he came out an hour later. I was crying so he hugged me, kissed me and sweet-talked me then drove me home.

I remember when we were hanging out and he fell asleep at the steering wheel and I didn't realize he was sleep until I looked up and we were on the opposite side of 111th street. His feet stepped all the way down on the pedal and we were speeding down the street on the wrong side of the road.

So, I immediately tried to get his foot off the gas pedal but his leg was so heavy, so I put the car in park which was a very dangerous thing. If your foot is on the gas pedal and you throw it into park, the engine could detach and be thrown back into your lap coming through the car. But it didn't happen and it was only God. I thank God every day that he protected me through all that time being with my husband. He ended up being just like Papa. I couldn't pick the right man if I tried.

Marvilyn's boyfriend's name was Daryl Wilson. And she got a lot of kids by him, I don't know how many. Before

she started having kids by him, we would all sit around the house and get high, drinking Bacardi rum. She already had Shawn and Aisha and Darryl was like the babysitter. When she got pregnant with Lil-D (Daryl Jr.), Daryl would stay home and just watch all the kids.

When my husband had got arrested one time and went to jail, and I was staying in the basement of Momma's house, Daryl came and forced his way in the back door and raped me in my own house. I was so messed up behind that because this was my sister's boyfriend, we would get high together. And this happened a few times, not just one time. I tried to tell my sister but she didn't want to believe me. And so, she finally did find out that it was true. She got mad, and after my husband got out of jail, she ended up having sex with my husband, told me about it, and left her underwear behind the dresser. Which I thought was so awful, terrible, but I forgave my husband for that.

Earl started fighting me, we now had physical altercations. He'd beat me up all the time, bust my lip, and all types of crazy shit when he got mad, and just wanted to go out. My Momma told me not to let him do me like that. I needed to draw blood from his ass so, I ended up fighting back. I was never really scared of him; it was just that I could not beat him. And I, oh my God, I thought I was reliving Papa again, that's how bad it was. But when my Momma told me, 'draw blood form his ass, he'll leave your ass alone,' that's what I did. I had started planting knives all over the house.

We were in the basement downstairs one night. He hit me and knocked me down on the couch. I had a hatchet, like a meat cleaver in the couch, and when I came up, I hit him with it across his hand. He still has the scar to this day. It almost took off his hand and of course, he ran out of the house, wrapped it up and called the police.

The police looked for me, I hid and eventually, he made up to me. But he did that just to get back into the house, and he called the police again which was a coupled weeks later. We ended up breaking up again.

He was still going in and out of jail and each time, I'd end up being a prostitute to support my drug habit. Then Momma decided to put a second mortgage on the house from Freelance mortgage company. I went down to sign the paperwork with her. We ended up getting a lot of money with that second mortgage. She supported my drug habit and didn't know it. I went from free-basing Cocaine to shooting Heroine.

I would just continue doing it after Earl went to jail. It was just me and my son at first till he got out, then I got pregnant with my daughter a year later. My daughter Ruth, she weighed 1 pound and 2 ounces when she was born. I loved her, but she reminded me of my husband so much who was at that time cheating and playing the field as well as going in and out of jail.

When I was pregnant with my daughter, my second child, I was talking to Earl out the window which was at ground level since I was in the basement. I was standing on a

chair, and he kicked me in the face and knocked me out the chair. I thought I would lose her but I didn't.

That night, I was laying on the couch after getting high all-night drinking beer, and alcohol. I had painted and did some stucco work earlier that evening. Momma came downstairs while I was putting stucco on the ceiling and she warned me not to do that because it would wrap up the umbilical cord around the baby's neck, but I ignored her and kept on working with the stucco on the ceiling.

Then I began to bleed, but my water didn't break. The baby was sitting on top of the placental, and I went into the hospital. They tried to induce labor but it was no good. I had a C-section and she came out premature. She had to stay in the hospital from August until November. After she came out. she had to have a nurse come around once a week. They all called her the miracle baby because she weighed 1 pound 2 ounces

After she was born, one time I got so strung out, I thought that I hated my daughter because she reminded me so much of her father, and I couldn't deal with her anymore. My daughter was very light-skinned when she was born just like his grandfather and his mother. I took her out back and left her under a truck for about 4 or 5 hours. She was just an infant. Then God put in my mind, what would happen if that truck ran over her? I had to run out there to get her.

Earl at first denied my child, and every time he'd get mad at me, he'd say that she wasn't his child, but she looks just like him and his people. When she was little, I didn't want

to have too much to do with her. He was in jail when she was born.

My Momma was renting out to Tasha, a drag queen. Her real name was Anthony Bakes. She saw me one day at the house and said,

"Hey girl what's up. Come on in."

"Okay."

I went into her apartment and we sat at the kitchen table together. As we were sitting there, she said,

"Girl, let me pull you up a drink. Want some of this Vodka?"

"Well you know I do. Shit… pour it up."

"Alright girl, you ain't said nothin' but a word. I got a whole fifth for us and got another gallon in the room."

"Alright, that sound's good. Let's do it."

After she poured, she went over to turn up the music she had on the record player. We started chit-chatting about stuff, you know small talk. Talking about men and maybe going out that night. We just continued to drink and talk shit.

All of a sudden, here comes Earl. He came out of her bedroom and didn't know that I was in the kitchen, and he only had his draws on.

"Goddam Tasha, you could a told me." He said as I jumped up.

"Told you what?" I yelled, "That I was over here? Ain't this a motha-fucking bitch. Ya'll, both ya'll mother-fucka's is trippin'. Ya'll ain't shit. Some no-good mother-fucka's" I said as I ran out the door running down the steps.

I was still talking when I got downstairs,

"Ya'll full of shit. I can't stand neither one of ya'll mother-fucka's. I hope both of ya'll fuck around and die."

I was so hurt. And, oh my God, I just ran out of the house. I knew that our relationship was over then because I knew that Tasha was not a woman, she was a man, she was a drag queen. So, from that point on, I did not want to be with him.

I knew there was something strange about him anyway because when we would have sex, he would always lay with his legs open and would ask me to stick my figure in his butt. And I knew there was something strange about that. And he would want me to play with his titties and I had never experienced that before. It was strange to me; nobody had ever asked me to do anything like that before. I know people do kinky sex, but I was amazed about it. I use to do it to please him but I didn't like doing it.

After this happened, I forgave Tasha because she was cool and I knew that it was all Earl's fault with his kinky ass. So, I was in the apartment with Tasha and noticed

that she had all my albums stacked up in her house. I was like,

"Goddam, ain't these my albums?"

The albums were 33 records and I had a lot of 'em because we use to get them out the paper for a penny from Motown and they would send them to us almost every week. I had every record that Motown ever put out. Not only did she have my records, and my candle stand from when Earl and I got married, but I saw other things that belonged to me in her apartment. They had been together for quite some time.

Earl and I would fight all the time after that. I had caught him with the drag queen so, he tried to get me back, but I wasn't biting. Every time he saw me, he wanted to fight. I went to Johnny's house one time. I thought he might help me after everything that was going on. I realized then that I was in love with Johnny because I had to refrain from running to him and jumping into his arms. But I was married, and I just couldn't. I came out of his place and Earl was waiting there for me. It seemed like he would wait for me outside everywhere I went. I made my mind up to go to Detroit, Mi to get away from him.

Momma got in the car to take me to the Greyhound station. I felt like I was running for my life. I knew Momma couldn't handle two kids and I knew Earl would use Irving, my son, to get back at me. This was the hardest thing in the world for me, but one thing I knew without a doubt, that he would help Momma with lil Ruth because she was a girl, and he wouldn't take her away

from Momma. I knew that just as sure as my name is
Ruth,

But he had no such misgivings about taken Irving though.
They didn't get along at all. My baby boy had stabbed his
father in the leg when he jumped on me once. He told his
father,

"You bet-not hit my mother or I will kill you."

I knew from that day on I had to get away not only for
my life but for my sons' life too. If I didn't go, someone
was going to get hurt so, Irving and I were on the run. I
had to leave my daughter behind. It was one of the
hardest things I'd ever had to do.

Chapter Nine: East to Detroit, Then Back to Chicago

So, my son and I were Greyhound bound to Detroit. The whole way I was looking out the window and crying, thinking about my daughter and all that I'd been through. We arrived in Detroit and my uncle Bubba and Aunt Ruth picked us up from the bus station. They were glad to see me. They gave me hugs and welcomed me with open arms. Aunt Ruth said,

"We're so glad you're here little one. You don't have to be abused anymore. All that's over now. You're here with us and we'll take care of you."

Uncle Bubba cut in, "That's right. You don't have to worry 'bout that nigga comin' here. We got something for 'em. He bed-not step to my door talking shit 'bout where's my wife. We won't have that here. Period!"

I was just so happy that somebody finally had my back at least. So, we go to the house and go inside. I had already been there before because some summers Mom and I would go visit and we'd stay with them for a week or two but, this time my Mom wasn't with me. I was there alone and I didn't know too much about them. Only that Uncle Bubba was my mother's brother. Come to find out later, they weren't blood-related.

Uncle Bubba and Aunt Ruth showed me to my room which was upstairs right down the hall from their room. Like they wanted to keep a good eye on me. It was nice

and big, Kenneth's old room. It had a nice big bed and I enjoyed it there because Irving was little and he was able to run around upstairs and everything.

Now Irving was meddlesome and after we'd been there for a week and everything was going well, he got into Kenneth's cologne which was called "Grey Flannel." It was really expensive at that time and very powerful. I didn't know what had happened. I started smelling this strong smell and as I got closer to Irving, I realized what he had done, he had gotten it all over himself.

I took him in to give him a bath to try to get this cologne off him, not realizing that he had spilled this man's cologne everywhere. I tried to get it up and hoped that Kenneth wouldn't see it. But of course, he did and got mad about it. I tried to tell him that it was an accident and that my son didn't mean to spill it. But he didn't care. I think that he thought that I was using it which made him pissed off about it.

As I stayed there, I tried to get on welfare for me and my child, especially to get food stamps and ADC – Aid to Dependent Children. I did, I got assistance from the state and got a little check. This was the first time I had received it on my own. Every other time I got a check like that, it was in my husband's name. When he went to jail a couple of times, I didn't even realize that he was getting this money until after he went to jail. He told me to go down to the exchange and get his foods stamps which he'd been getting all along without my knowledge

So, I was finally able to switch everything over to my name where I could get food stamps and a little check. That was helping me and Irving out to buy food and clothes. Uncle Bubba didn't charge me rent or anything right then. He wanted me to get a job though so, I went out and started looking for something to help pay the bills, and stuff like that.

But I was very young. I was only 17 years old at the time. I didn't know anything about working or anything like that. So, as I began to look for work, I really couldn't find anything because I didn't have any type of education or experience. I talked to him about sharing my food stamps. In Detroit, you got them twice a month so I asked him if I could share one of the food stamps with him and then the 2nd one I'd keep for me and Irving. I would also give him half of my check for ADC.

He was agreeable and said he wouldn't charge me any money but I could help to put food in the house. Irving and I weren't eating there often, but sometimes we did so I didn't have any objections to this.

Aunt Ruth and Uncle Bubba started talking about possibly moving me down to the basement where they kept their dog at the time. It was huge, almost like a house within itself but I'd have to clean up the dog shit if I were to move down there. I wanted it though because it would have been great for me and Irving. I'd even started cleaning it, but I never got a chance to move down there.

They use to have big parties, card parties on Friday and Saturday nights. Aunt Ruth wanted me to cook chicken

and serve it and stuff. And I did it, but I didn't know that I was supposed to collect some extra money by doing this. I was supposed to charge them for the plate. Then they'd give you a tip to serve them drinks and stuff like that. I was just giving away the food because no one had explained it to me.

Aunt Ruth got upset with me and scolded me badly about this. Card parties were to make money, not just to give away all the food and everything. They would play Bid Whist and Spades for money. I didn't know anything about gambling at the time. But they broke me in real fast. And the next time that they had a card party, I was on my way. I was serving food and drinks and I made a lot of money.

While I stayed with them my drug habit went down. I wasn't doing Cocaine or anything, just drinking. But I was drinking heavy. Then I met her daughter Jackie. I went over to her house one weekend, come to find out, Jackie was getting' high. That was the first time I got introduced to what they called "Rock" Cocaine.

They were doing Rock in Detroit, they weren't cooking it up, it was already in the rock format so, all you had to do was put it in this stem. I didn't know anything about it because in Chicago we were still cooking it and using pipes; we were still free-basing. When I gave her my $50.00 and she brought all these small bags back, I said,

"What the hell is this?"

I thought it was that new drug, Ice or something, I didn't know what it was. But it was good. It was kinda like Cocaine but with a little better taste to it. I was like,

"Hey, okay."

So, I started to do Rock Cocaine, and she was the one who introduced me to that. Every weekend, whenever they had the card parties, I would go to her house and spend the night getting' high.

One weekend, I went over there and Jackie had been bleeding from her vagina and she wasn't on her period. She was having a miscarriage because she was pregnant but, she didn't want me to tell her parents. She was getting high, and me being the person that I am, like, I hate to see people suffer, and I didn't want anything to happen to her, so I told Uncle Bubba and Aunt Ruth.

They rushed over there and I had to tell them that she was using, which I probably shouldn't have. It's probably the biggest mistake of my life because once they found out that she was using, they knew that I also was using and they didn't want that shit around them. No matter what I did, they didn't want it around them.

All of a sudden, they would find little things wrong with me or they'd find things like socks missing and things like that to blame me for. People will find things to use against you when they find out things about you that they don't like.

Next thing you know, Uncle Bubba's daughter, Michelle, said that I liked her and was watching her. She told this to

her husband too and the whole thing started feeling uncomfortable enough that finally her husband and I got into it. He tossed me out of the house. When Uncle Bubba got back, he told him that he shouldn't have done that, but at the same time, he told me that he thought it was time that I went back to Chicago.

My son and I stayed there for about 5 and a half months. They brought another Greyhound bus ticket for us, I packed up our little stuff, and the next thing you know, we were on our way back to Chicago. Back to some more turmoil.

When I got there, Tony and Cynthia had moved in downstairs, and Aunt Dot returned to the middle part of the house back from the Gardens. Momma was sleeping on the couch, and here comes me and my son. Aunt Dot did move back upstairs for a little while, so the house was full, but then eventually, they ended up moving back out again getting another place down the street.

My relationship with Earl was over, and so I was drinking heavy then. Every time he saw me, Momma was still giving me money every day to supply my drug habit. So, I'd go to the liquor store to get some liquor and he'd be there. I don't know if he would follow me or what but he'd show up and chase me. He would threaten me, I always had a hard time getting back to the car. At one time I even chased him with the car because he made me so mad.

Finally, He didn't seem to want to have anything to do with me anymore. The last time he went to jail it was for

about 2 and a half years and I was steady getting high all the time. I felt like everything that happened to me in that house with all the rapes, and molestations, and people chasing me home from school, the only thing I felt I was good at was doing drugs so, I continued to do it.

At the same time, I was pushing the only person that loved me, my mother, away from me because money was getting low and I had almost spent up all the money we got from the second mortgage. She was getting social security and the house was paid for, but how was she paying the lights and the gas bills. I was going through all the money we had and I would push her to go out in the middle of the night to borrow money from people.

She was getting old and tired but I still would push her to do this. She would go to the bank and get out $50.00 to $100.00 at a time and give me that, but I still wasn't happy because I would go right through it. I would try to send her out at 12 midnight or 1 a.m. to one of her church friends houses to borrow money for me, cause by this time I had both a Cocaine, and Heroin addiction, and I didn't see any way out, and I had 2 kids.

My Mom eventually got sick and tired of me throwing my life away, so she left me and went to Detroit. I couldn't believe that she left me in the house alone with 2 kids knowing I was a dope fiend and Heroin addict. I couldn't take care of those 2 children, she knew that. But I had run her away, and I continued with my drug habit, not even feeding, clothing, and bathing them. I would give them cough syrup to put them to sleep, then leave

them in the house alone to go get dope. They were 2 and 3 years old.

I would tell my son to go to the store and steal yourself some potato chips or some bologna or something to eat. Tasha would take them sometimes to feed them because she knew that they didn't have anything to eat. My sister Marvilyn stayed in some apartments across town by this time. I was like, why wouldn't she come to help me with my children? Especially since I helped her when her children were babies. She could buy them clothes and stuff. Why wouldn't anybody come to help me? Even Reverend Meeks wouldn't come over.

As my addiction kept on progressing, I couldn't see my way out. Marvilyn came over one night and I gave her some money to get my children some White Castles and she said she would so she took my money. Then I asked my play brother Jerry to get me $25.00 worth of Cocaine and $25.00 worth of Heroin. I waited on Marvilyn all night to come back, and I waited all night for Jerry to come back with the drugs, but both of them ran away with my money.

My mother told the people who were renting from her, to pay the rent so my kids would have something to eat, and I would have some money in my pocket. But the people wouldn't pay me the rent, so, I was so mad and hurt with them, and I had these kids, and I didn't know what to do, so I just wanted to die. I just wanted to Fuck the world.

I came up with this plan. I am going out with a big bang. I set the house on fire with me and my two kids inside of

it. But just in the nick of time, I came to my senses and got my two kids out. I put them in a shopping cart and went over to a friend's house.

This is not the end of the story, there's another book to come. Because you know what happened next, I ended up in prison.

Made in the USA
Columbia, SC
04 September 2022